DONKEY PACK

by
Laura Leveque a

Donkey Packing Basics
Part 1

~

After you've had an encounter with a donkey on a walking tour, had real contact with one, you're never the same. You're somehow touched forever.
—Andy Merrifield, *The Wisdom of Donkeys*

~

In January 2009, while wintering in Deming, New Mexico, I received and replied to a series of e-mails from Pat (aka Cow-Patty) about donkey packing. Her questions about donkey packing were common questions I'd received over the years from readers, so I am going to answer them here, as best as I can.

The first e-mail read: "I met you a couple years ago when your consignment store 'Jackass Junction' was open in Deming. I was in the process of moving from Texas to New Mexico with my horse, mule, and donkey. Now I want to plan some pack trips with my donkey and have lots of questions. I've read your articles in *The Brayer* magazine so I figured you are the expert on donkey packing, so I'm writing you. Cow-Patty"

"Dear Cow-Patty. Good to hear from you! Yes, I've done lots of donkey packing. I learned by doing it for eighteen years and by studying books like *Horses, Hitches, and Rocky Trails*, by Joe Back. I'd be glad to give you my opinion to any questions you have. Jackass Jill"

"Jill, I'll probably have tons of questions later, but will start with a few now. A little background . . . this fall my neighbor took me on a two night pack trip. There were three people with mounts and one packhorse. I carried all my stuff on my mule and my neighbor hauled the cooking gear. So, that is my total experience.

"My husband Dave, aka the Professor, is retiring in May, and he doesn't ride, but is interested in hiking, camping, and mineral collecting, and I want him to see these really neat places I found while riding. Soooo, now I want to pack in with my donkey.

"So far I'm just walking her on the side of the road with the packsaddle on . . . no load.

"I've attached a couple pics of my donkey. I'm guessing she's between 400-425 pounds. She's about four years old. How much weight would you put on her? How do you tie them at night? Do you hobble yours? Should I use special smaller size hobbles or regular size? I saw some donkey hobbles advertised and wondered...have you ever tried a single hobble? Have you used an overhead tie set-up? And do you use panniers? I have a big saddlebag that the local saddle-maker said he thought would work okay for now. Pat and Mouse"

"Pat, All my pack donkeys were/are standard to large standard size, 500 + pounds. Men and women, including myself (weights up to 190 lbs) have ridden the donkeys for two to three hours. When I rode longer hours I'd ride a mile or two then walk a mile. They can carry more live weight than dead weight. The weight I carry on my donkeys depends on how far and type of terrain. Your donkey, Mouse, is smaller than my donkeys, so I'd start with some day trips, with 50-60 pounds. Then gradually work up to 75 to100 pounds in well-balanced soft or hard panniers and top pack. Jill"

Type of Panniers and Weight

I'll give some examples of balancing panniers in Part 2. If the pack is too heavy, or there is rubbing or discomfort, a donkey will often stop and let you know.

If your donkey is young and frisky, like Pat's jennet Mouse, and the weight you have isn't slowing your donkey down, and you are exhausted from holding your donkey back, it might be a good idea to add more weight, like two or three extra gallons of water on each side.

I've used soft panniers in dense woods to reduce snagging, but I prefer hard panniers for a number of reasons: more even pressure and weight on the packsaddle then on the donkey's ribs; no protrusions into the donkey's sides; contents of packs more stable and less likely to get smashed and leak; there is a more stable secure platform for the top-pack where sleeping bags, tents, cots, etc., are stacked. You can also carry more drinking water. When at camp the pack boxes can be used as a table and chair, and can be placed inside the tent to weigh it down when it gets windy, and to act as a bedside table.

~

(**Note**: Some professional horse and mule packers prefer heavy canvas panniers instead of hard-sided panniers because they are safer for the pack animal if he falls and safer if the animal panics and thwacks another pack animal or person. Wrecks are less likely with a pack string of donkeys than with mules and horses.)

~

Pat asked, "Do you use standard horse-size panniers? Do you know a good site to find used pack gear? I was looking for donkey Utah panniers, but haven't found any used ones. Hadn't thought of all the pros of hard panniers.

"I've attached some pics of my second outing with Mouse. Not as smooth as the first outing. Pat"

"Pat, When I saw your pictures I had a good belly laugh. They brought donkey training memories. I remember Willy, my grey-dun donkey, having fits over six inch wide trickles of water, but Shaggy, my spotted donkey, and I ignored his frantic pawing and braying and kept on walking, eventually Willy would leap over the trickle of water as if it were a six-foot wide trench filled with snapping crocodiles, and catch up to us. Jill"

Pat training Mouse. Mouse getting accustomed to her new packsaddle and new job.

MORE ABOUT PANNIERS

I got my panniers at a used tack auction in Washington state 20 years ago. Both sets are plywood.

The large panniers are 11" wide at the base and 14" wide on the top, and 24" lengthwise, and 18" tall. This set of panniers has a slight curve on the inside where it rests against the saddle. I use this set on Shaggy, my big boned, 600 + pound donkey. These panniers are too long for Willy the smaller boned, shorter backed donkey.

The smaller panniers are square plywood boxes covered in canvas and leather; 10 1/2" wide, 22 1/2" long, 14 1/2" tall. These are the pony/burro sized boxes.

(Tip: use a Horse and Pony Height-Weight Tape, mine is made by the Coburn Co. By measuring your donkey's heart girth you get an estimate of your donkey's size.)

Donkey packing gear.

Handsome Shaggy with wood panniers.

Pat asked, "Should I buy some 'Utah Panniers'? I'm going to the saddle shop next week and will look at the panniers. I can find Utah Panniers for $105. Is that reasonable?

I told Pat, "I believe Utah canvas panniers also come in a donkey size, and probably a bit more expensive. The standard horse/mule size Utah panniers may be too long and can press on the kidney hip area. (If the bags are too long, you could run a strap lengthwise around the pannier to pull the weight and corner away from her hip. Sometimes it's just a matter of a few inches.) If you can get panniers for $105 seems like a good price. Utah panniers are nice looking, light, (made of canvas and leather) and easy to use, from what I've seen, though they don't have a cover flap. Most the panniers I looked at were $300-$500, but they were the aluminum and hard plastic type."

~

(Pannier is a French derived word for basket. Panniers are sometimes called panyards, kyacks, alforjas, saddle bags, or just plain old pack boxes.)

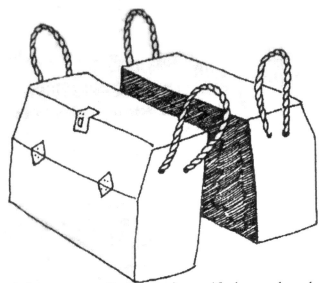

Pack boxes are called: panniers, alforjas, or kyacks

Panniers

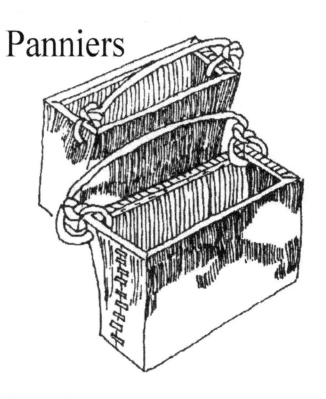

PACKSADDLES

I get occasional e-mails or letters asking about types and sizes of packsaddles. Most donkey and pony packers, including myself, mainly use the sawbuck packsaddles. Sawbucks have wood cross-pieces front and back, and carved wood side bars. The sawbuck normally come fully rigged with double cinches, breast collar, and britchen (sometimes spelled britchin) or breeching (butt strap), and is available in standard donkey and miniature donkey sizes. The Decker packsaddle has metal loops and padded pack boards and can withstand trail wrecks and carry heavier loads than a sawbuck. It's used by the Forest Service to haul fence posts and bags of concrete into remote areas. The Decker has only one cinch and I've never seen donkey or pony sizes available, and is more expensive than the sawbuck.

Cow Patty found a donkey size sawbuck packsaddle on eBay for her small standard donkey, Mouse. She ordered packing gear from PackSaddleShop.com and Southern Missouri Mule Co., SoMoMule.com.

At PackSaddleShop.com, on the Pannier Purchasing Guide page, they listed Salt Panniers as being suitable for smaller equines.

A typical sawbuck packsaddle. Because the cinches are too short for this donkey, it'd be best to either pad the lower cinch rings or get longer cinches.

Finding the Correct Size Gear

Finding packing supplies for small standard to large standard donkeys is not too difficult, even minis have good suppliers, but in-between sized donkeys have to be custom fitted with packsaddles.

An example is Leigh Anne's donkey, Jasmine. She is 38 inches tall; a size between a mini and a small standard. The mini packsaddle was too small; the donkey packsaddle too big. Leigh Anne and Jasmine hike the trails of Saguaro National Park as Trail Patrol Unit volunteers, so she needed appropriate gear. We e-mailed back and forth a few times and I suggested trying a youth or pony saddle as a packsaddle or have the paddles on a donkey sawbuck cut-down and reshaped. She did find a master wood worker to design a sawbuck packsaddle based on a size between the mini sawbuck and the standard donkey sawbuck.

When I had more donkeys than packsaddles I'd sling soft panniers, matching suitcases, or duffel bag pairs over western youth, pony, McClellan, and cordura saddles that I rigged-up or had a saddle maker add another cinch and britchin' to. (Britchin' is sometimes spelled britchen', with or without the '.) I normally don't bother with a breast collar, a donkey's pot bellied build keeps the saddle from slipping forward, even on the steepest trails, though a breast collar makes the pack animal look well dressed. When in doubt about fit add an extra saddle pad and pack less weight.

~

Study the drawings in *Horses, Hitches, and Rocky Trails*, and you'll be able to pack and manty just about anything on just about any type of saddle.

Decker packsaddle

The Decker is used primarily on full size horses and
mules for extra heavy loads.

~

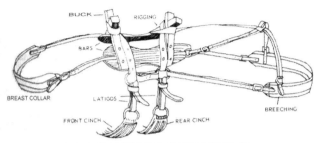

BUCK — RIGGING

BARS

BREAST COLLAR

LATIGOS

BREECHING

FRONT CINCH — REAR CINCH

SAWBUCK PACKSADDLE

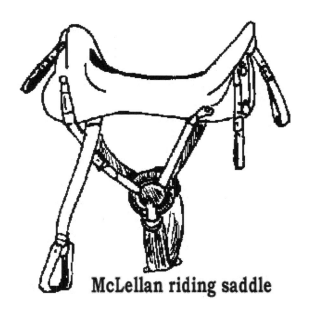

McLellan riding saddle

When I used the McLellan for riding or packing a donkey, I rigged it with double cinches and a britchen, instead of the single cinch shown here.

CAMPING WITH YOUR DONKEY

Keeping your Donkey in Camp

Hobbles

The first two years when I packed the donkeys I tried every method I'd read about or saw used by other packers. With hobbles, both single and double, seems no matter how much padding I put on the hobbles, even donkey size hobbles, they always caused sores on their pasterns. So I don't use them. If you are camping for only a few days they'd be fine, but I was camping for sometimes months at a time.

Staking

I've successfully staked out the donkeys on thirty foot lines. I alternate one donkey loose and the rest staked, but staking requires numerous nighttime checks for tangling. Overhead tying is okay and there is a lot less tangling in the lines, but finding trees set apart without a bunch of scrub in between, or any trees at all, for two to six animals is sometimes difficult, and the forage gets eaten and stomped down in a matter of hours. Also it's hard for the donkeys to roll without getting a line twisted around their necks.

Bells

Another technique is attaching bells to the donkeys' halters and turning them loose, then finding them in the morning. This works okay with three of four people available to search and catch them, but I don't recommend it with only one or two people.

Electric Polywire Corrals

My favorite method that I use almost exclusively is a single strand of polywire fencing with a solar powered or battery powered fence charger, a dozen or so plastic step-in posts, and 300 foot roll of polywire. (Polywire and polytape is made of poly threads woven together with thin wire into what looks like either a roll of thick string or a roll of ribbon.)

Polywire and polytape is available in varying length rolls. Because my donkeys are trained to respect a single strand of polywire, I sometimes don't use the fence charger. I can run the polywire from bush to bush or tree, and use two step-in posts for the gate (though this isn't necessary). I move this portable corral as needed. When training a new donkey to a polywire corral I use two strands of polywire or polytape and lots of plastic step-in posts. The larger the corral the better.

A donkey camp, using two strands of polytape and a
battery powered fence charger.

After fifteen years of use, my solar fence charger died, so I bought a small battery operated charger with a built-in ground rod. It fits in a lunch box. It's called The Pegasus, HP-B124 by Horse Power, available through FarmTek.com. In order for your portable electric fence to work properly you need a good ground stake or rod. A one-and-a-half to two-foot metal rod is plenty. The trick is keeping the dirt around the ground rod damp. Dump your coffee dregs and wash water at the ground rod.

To set-up the portable electric corral I space the step-in plastic or fiberglass posts every 10-15 feet in as large an area as I have posts for. The boundaries can be in a round, rectangular, or any shape depending on terrain. I decide where the gate will be and set 2 posts side by side. Then tie the end of my polywire or polytape to the top of one of these gate posts, then go around the fence perimeter, away from the gate post, attaching the polywire/tape to the top of the fence posts.

When I reach the other gate post I secure it at the top, then I secure or tie the tape/wire to the center of that gate post I head back the way I came attaching the wire to the posts at the same level making a two strand corral. I end-up at the same post I started with. I don't cut my polywire/tape roll at this point, but I stick it on the top a post or put the roll on the ground on something plastic to insulate it from grounding out.

Now it's time to attach the fence charger. I drive a spike or ground rod a foot or so into the ground, and soak the ground at the ground rod with water, then I attach the ground clip to the ground rod and attach the (hot) clip to the polywire/tape, then turn it on. I use a fence tester or listen for the click-click sound.

I recommend testing your fence and getting your animals use to electric fencing before leaving home on an expedition. When I know the fence is working I turn off the charger or unhook the positive hot wire clip, move one of the gate posts leaving an opening to bring the donkeys in the new corral and releasing them. This corral can be expanded and/or moved whenever needed. (See diagram.)

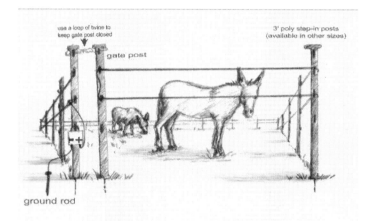

use a loop of twine to
keep gate post closed

gate post

3' poly step-in posts
(available in other sizes)

ground rod

PACKING IN FEED

Rather than packing in hay or grain I found the non-alfalfa hay cubes or pellets a good alternative. The high protein in alfalfa is not necessary for donkeys. There are 100% grass hay pellets available. I've used Bermuda, orchard grass, and timothy grass pellets successfully in areas where there is no edible vegetation or as a treat to keep them nearby. As my donkeys got into their twenties, I had to start wetting down their pellets, otherwise my donkeys would choke on the dry pellets. Choke is rarely fatal, but is uncomfortable for the donkeys, and can look quite scary to the wrangler.

Donkey Packing Basics Part 2

PAT AND MOUSE'S FIRST PACK TRIP

The weather that February was sunny so I wrote, "Pat, In the next few weeks might be fun to take all the donkeys on a day hike, with lunch, and cameras. Your donkey might learn a lot by following my donkeys, particularly Shaggy, over and around obstacles. My spotted (paint colored) donkey, Shaggy, by example, helped me train at least eight other donkeys, plus his buddy Willy, to be led, saddled and ridden, and to carry packs, to ride in a trailer, cross water, go over bridges, and stay calm no matter what scary thing happens."

Pat replied, "I know a great place for a first trial-run with Mouse and her pack. It's a two-and-a-half mile trail leading to the Big Tree in the Gila National Forest."

I wrote back, "Let's go!"

Big Tree Trailhead

I met Pat and Mouse at the Big Tree Trailhead, both of us had our stock trailers. As Pat (aka Cow-Patty once known as Mule Lady when she raised mules in Texas and competed in Endurance events with her riding mule in New Hampshire, Virginia, California, Texas, and New Mexico; I wasn't dealing with someone new to handling stock.)

So after we brushed our donkeys to get dirt and stickers off, and made sure our saddle pads were free of anything scratchy, I put the saddle blankets and double-cinched sawbuck packsaddles on Shaggy and

Willy. Before tightening the girth cinches I lift the saddle pad/blanket away from the animal's spine and withers. By putting my hand and wrist into the space below the saddle bucks and under the pad, I lift the pad making a kind of tunnel and air space above the spine.

I told Pat that I always tighten the breeching harness before I finish tightening the girth cinches leaving the rear girth cinch a bit looser. I leave the breast collar loose or remove it; I've never found it necessary on donkeys. Then I showed Pat how tight the breeching or britchin' (butt strap) should be to stop the cinch from sliding too close to the front legs and causing gall sores.

I said, "If your pack animal's cinch is rubbing behind the front legs, tighten-up your breeching."

When you start out on the trail you may think your donkey's breeching and front girth cinch are too tight, but they will loosen as you walk. If you've hiked a half-hour or so and your donkey's breeching is tight as a straight jacket, it's time to loosen it a notch or two on both sides.

Balancing the Panniers

The next important thing I demonstrated was balancing the panniers. Pat had the lightweight canvas Utah panniers. I brought out my spring scale, and lined-up my four plywood panniers, then I started adding items to the boxes: tie-out ropes, poncho, coat, lunch, two short shovels, gold pans, extra lead rope and halter, roll of duct tape, etc. Later I'd add the 8 one-gallon water jugs, and four water bottles.

Using the spring-scale I put the pannier sling

ropes on the scale hook, and used both hands, with much grunting and groaning, lifted the loaded box, I checked the weight of one pannier against the other, transferring items as needed. I try to get each pannier set balanced to within a half-pound. The pannier that carries the spring scale needs to be two pounds lighter than its matching pannier. Then I emptied each side of the panniers into plastic garbage bags in separate piles. I slung the empty boxes over the bucks of the packsaddle. (In my younger days I'd lift full panniers onto the packsaddle, now I think hefting seventy to eighty pound panniers ridiculous.) Once the empty panniers were on the donkeys, I loaded the water. On this short trip I used gallon jugs instead of flat, hard-sided three gallon cans. I put two gallons of water into each pannier, plus a water bottle, then added the bagged-up pre-weighed loads into each designated pannier.

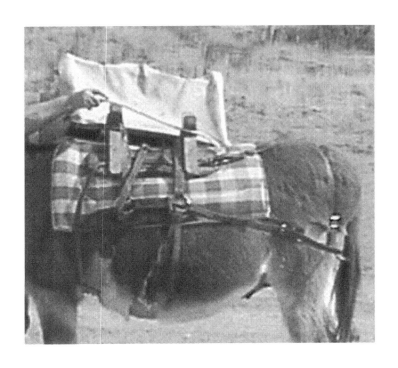

Shaggy and Willy at the trailhead.

~

Mouse at the trailhead with Utah panniers and carrying camp gear and plastic step-in posts.

Then Pat loaded and balanced her canvas panniers. We did some minor breeching adjustments, I put my scale in the light pannier, we locked our vehicles and hit the trail, with Shaggy and I in the lead, followed by Willy, then Pat and Mouse.

On our first trip I left my dog, Joey, at home. I thought Mouse might be too nervous on her first outing to tolerate a dog.

Mouse jumped around a little bit, not used to all the stuff hanging on her back, but with Pat's calm, assertive handling, Mouse settled into a nice pace.

On the Trail

We hiked through mixed stands of piñon pine, and Gambel's oak, and into and out of small rocky canyons in the foothills of the Pinos Altos Range in Fort Bayard's Elk Refuge. (Fort Bayard was an 1860s U.S. Infantry Post.)

The trail dropped to a broad, waist-high grassy valley dotted with towering cottonwoods. We passed a convergence of trails where deep wagon ruts are still visible: the Sawmill Wagon Road, Wood Haul Wagon Trail, and our route, The Big Tree Trail fork.

After a few water, pack adjustment, and pee breaks we got to the Big Tree.

The Big Tree is the second largest alligator juniper in the United States. The 600 year old tree is over 18 feet around and 63 feet high.

I unloaded my panniers, lifted them off the donkeys' packsaddles and set them down next to the giant tree to act as seats and tables. I loosened Shaggy's and Willy's cinches and staked the donkeys out on thirty foot lines. Pat unloaded Mouse and loosened her cinch.

Mouse flung her head, brayed, paced in circles, and got tangled in her long-line, so Pat tied the line up high and snug.

We offered all the donkeys water. After lunch we explored the glades around the Big Tree; we found a stream. It was getting late and we wanted to be out before dark, so we repacked and ambled back to the trailhead.

PAT AND MOUSE'S SECOND PACK TRIP

In early March we met again at the trailhead with the three donkeys, and my dog Joey. I brought along my 12-volt electric fence charger packed safely in a lunch bucket, a roll of polywire, and dozen step-in plastic posts that I strapped to Shaggy's top pack. I'd demo the portable corral so Pat could see how easy it was to set-up and Mouse could do a little grazing this time.

Our pack train went past the Big Tree to the cottonwood lined stream bank. Shaggy and I led the way. We slipped and slid down the bank; panniers and gear flopping, banging, and snagging on branches. All of us except Joey got mud splattered. On the other side we set-up our picnic area in a small meadow edged by a stand of oak.

Joey whined and sniffed at some day-old bear blob (poop) next to our picnic spot. If we planned to spend the night we'd have to move camp away from this game trail, but we'd be gone before dusk, so it was okay to stay here. Joey and I checked around for any suspicious stick and dirt piles that might be covering a recent kill made by a mountain lion or bear; in that case we'd need to leave the area quickly. Joey didn't find anything.

We both watched the three donkeys grazing peacefully, and Joey lying down. I told Pat, "If Joey and the donkeys were startled by anything, they'd let us know."

Another reason I preferred using the portable corral when camping in remote areas is a hungry or angry bear or lion can injure and kill a staked-out or tethered animal much easier than a group of donkeys or mules in a collapsible corral. Mules and donkeys will fight back, and can move around and get some good kicks and bites in. An electric polywire fence will not stop them from getting out in an emergency. I can sleep soundly knowing my donkeys can roll, and graze, and run if necessary and not get tangled in lines.

The few times I've had bears come through camp, knocking down the portable fence. The dogs stayed in my tent growling and barking, while the donkeys rather than dash down the mountain side like a bunch of spooked horses, instead, rushed to my tent braying. Sometimes I think they knew I had the gun. This scenario rarely happens, but I was living pretty much year round at remote mine sites.

We lunched leisurely on that cool, but sunny March afternoon. A light breeze brought the smell of pines, and we listened to the donkeys pulling and munching dry grass and the trickling sound of nearby slow moving water. I unpacked my shovels and gold pans, and Cow-Patty and I went down to the stream for some lessons in panning, which she'd later share with the Professor. The stream had too much overburden to dig-up on a short afternoon. To find gold we'd need to stay a few days, search for a cut-bank or a toppled cottonwood and dig under the roots. Our purpose this time wasn't a prospecting expedition, but a donkey packing practice stroll.

When the sun dipped low and the tree shadows lengthened, we repacked our donkeys. Our pack train side slipped down to the stream, jumped across, scrambled up the opposite bank, and headed toward the main trail.

Mouse, the jennet pranced with energy, impatient

with me and my slow moving donkeys, so at the end of the second outing we tried Mouse in the lead. She seemed more relaxed out front and no longer afraid to cross wet spots and ravines. I watched Pat and Mouse move briskly ahead; after two outings Pat and Mouse looked and moved like experienced packers.

That summer Pat and the Professor went on a few pack trips with Mouse. Cow-Patty and the Professor became so enamored with donkeys that Pat bought Possum, a Mammoth riding and pack donkey. She and the Professor are talking about selling her endurance mule so he can get his own Mammoth riding and pack donkey. On their trips the Professor looks for minerals and pans for gold. Thanks to Shaggy's and Willy's example Pat and the Professor are now officially donkey packers and prospectors.

~

My treasures do not clink together or glitter;
They gleam in the sun and bray in the night.
—Desert Proverb

Pat and Mouse on the trial.

~

Willy was tied, in the above photo, with a six-foot dog lead to an O-ring on the top of Shaggy's britchin' harness using a single hitch. The recommended way to tie your pack string together is adding a short length of ¼ inch sisal, manila, cotton rope or any type rope or twine that will break-away in case of an emergency. On seldom-used trails and when I'm away from any roads, I lead Shaggy and let Willy follow untied.

MORE PACKING TIPS

Saddle Blankets

Most packers use the extra-long packsaddle blankets that reach almost to the equine's elbows for padding under the cinch rings and all the extra buckles, straps, and fastenings on a packsaddle, but I found for most standard and small standard size donkeys these extra-long blankets a bit too large. I use a thick rectangular horse-size saddle pad. The best type of saddle pad/blanket to use is much debated. I've used horse-hair, synthetic fleece, wool, and sheepskin. I buy whatever I can afford then use it as a dog bed or throw it away when it gets worn or matted.

Some professional packers hate horse-hair saddle blankets. My thought is that most professional packers use horses, and horses sweat a lot more than donkeys, so certain materials in saddle pads might cause sores in horses. Also professional pack stock often carry 200 lb loads and travel 15-25 miles per day, five to six days per week, for six to eight months out of the year, so their gear and tack requirements are different than hobby or part-time packers.

To Shoe or Not to Shoe

Most professional pack stock are shod. I've never had or needed shoes on my donkeys. My pack donkeys have their hooves trimmed as needed. Can be anywhere from every three to six months or only once a year, depending on the terrain they live or work on. Most pack donkeys aren't used enough to warrant shoeing. Historically mine donkeys and cart donkeys that worked long hours, often six or seven days a week, needed to be shod.

A Few More Packing Questions

Another donkey owner named Lee Ana, mailed me with questions that her dad (who has a donkey but no computer) had about packsaddles, which her dad referred to as crossbucks. I told her that my donkeys use sawbuck packsaddles. (Same as the crossbuck.) I bought these over 18 years ago and can't remember where I got them. They were special made to fit the shorter donkey back. A mule packsaddle is far too long and large and will press against the donkey's kidneys and obstruct movement in the hind legs.

A packsaddle or riding saddle made for a pony works. Before I found correct fitting packsaddles I used 13 inch western saddles and Mclellan Cavalry saddles and slung soft panniers over these saddles, worked quite well. I still do this sometimes.

The Western Pack Burro Association, 11023 Hwy 291, Salida, CO 81201, will know where you can get a donkey sawbuck packsaddle. The most important thing about donkeys and any type of saddle is the donkey has a tendency to have a potbelly and no withers to hold the saddle and cinches in place, and the front cinch will rub behind the front legs and gall the animal. With a donkey or any pot bellied equine with no withers you MUST use a britchin'. This is the strap that goes across the equine's butt to hold the saddle and cinch from moving too far forward. I always use two cinches, front and back, and add a britchin'. I've never seen a packsaddle without double cinches or britchin'.

The book *Horses, Hitches, and Rocky Trails* shows you how to sling a pack on a riding saddle, and everything you need to know about packing, including the different type of packsaddles: the sawbuck, the Decker, etc. Recently I saw an ad in I think it was a Wyoming Outdoors catalog, for a packsaddle made from plastic, and everything adjusted to fit any shaped back, though it was quite expensive. I prefer the look of the old fashioned wood crossbuck packsaddle.

When Shaggy, the spotted donkey was in his twenties he got rather barrel shaped. He had used a particular McClellan saddle for 15 years. It no longer fit him at all. It sat on his back like a child's hat on 300 lb football player's head. It was hysterical. When I tried to sneak a nice fitting cordura saddle with a broad tree on him, he would try to take it off and refused to move until I put his old saddle on. So I added an extra saddle pad to reduce pressure spots and kept both cinches and britchin' snug, and he was happy. His sawbuck packsaddle always fit him okay for the 18 years he wore it. Sometimes adding an extra pad can help the problem of not-so-perfect saddles.

A final word about balancing panniers: The few times I failed to weigh my panniers I paid for with many lost hours stopping to adjust and re-adjust the panniers and slipping packsaddle. If your panniers are balanced, your cinches can loosen and your panniers and packed goods will arrive at your destination intact.

The following is good advice about using a scale to balance your load from Joe Back who wrote, "Balance the two sides of each pack . . . whether they're panniers, side packs . . . mantied cargo . . . or any daggoned ordinary pack you load. And say, Bud, you'll be surprised how much of a liar the scales make you out to be, no matter how good a guesser you think you are."

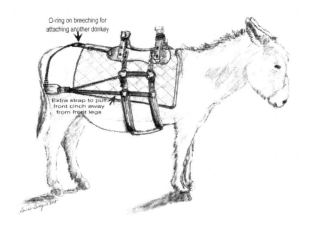

O-ring on breeching for attaching another donkey

Extra strap to pull front cinch away from front legs

For long pack trips you will probably use a top pack, a sling rope, and a lash cinch. A lash cinch is a third cinch, usually made of heavy duty, wide webbing, with a cinch ring on one end, and a hook on the other. The lash cinch goes under your donkey's belly, normally between and on top of the saddle cinches. You secure and tie the diamond hitch to the lash cinch. The diamond hitch stabilizes the top pack and panniers. So you may want to learn to throw a diamond hitch.

You can practice indoors using twine and a plastic model horse, or put your packsaddle and panniers on a sawhorse. Again I suggest you find a copy of *Horses, Hitches, and Rocky Trails*, and study the diamond hitches. I use the single diamond hitch because it was the easiest one for me to learn and use on my own, and it works much better than using bungee cords or netting to secure the top load

Pat and The Professor's Mammoth donkey, Moose, with top pack. A diamond hitch is optional with this type of equipment; though I'd probably use one if the trail was rugged.

SINGLE DIAMOND HITCH

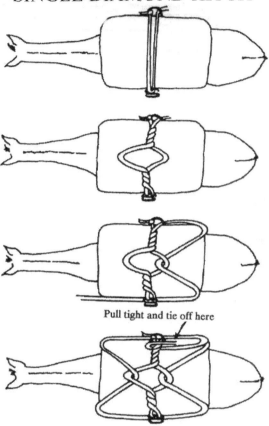

Pull tight and tie off here

The author with Shaggy and Willy. The donkeys have top packs, each secured by a single diamond hitch.

Jill with her donkeys, Shaggy and Willy.

A pack trip in the Peloncillo Mountains of New
Mexico. Texas Jack followed by Shaggy, Willy, and
Sarita. Accompanied by Soapy, the mine dog.

Resources

http://www.packsaddleshop.com

http://www.somomule.com

American Donkey and Mule Society
www.lovelongears.com

About the author:

Laura Leveque aka Jackass Jill was a columnist for *Gold Prospectors* magazine, and wrote the "Donkey Prospector" column from 1996 to 2011. The "Donkey Prospector" column was reprinted in *The Brayer* magazine. Leveque is also a landscape painter and illustrator. Some of her work can be seen at www.jackassjunction.net. Her book, *Whoa you donkey . . . WHOA! Adventures of a Lady Prospector*, and her other books are available through Amazon.

Joey and Willy

Printed in Great Britain
by Amazon